THE

CHIP

Paul and Carolyn Wilde

"And he causeth all, both small and great, rich and poor, free and bond, to receive a mark IN their right hand, or IN their foreheads."
REVELATION 13:16

Could the changing of just 1 letter in a two letter word cause men to fearlessly accept the mark that will result in their eternal doom? Nearly every version of the Bible changes the word "in" to "on" or "upon". This is a good time to check the Bible version you read.

All Scripture quotations are taken from the King James Version of the Bible.

"The words of the LORD are pure words: as silver tried in a furnace of earth, purified seven times. Thou shalt keep them, O LORD, thou shalt preserve them from this generation for ever."
PSALM 12:6-7

TABLE OF CONTENTS

THE WAIL OF A SIREN

Anyone who uses a computer understands that he can purchase a program online, and within seconds, install it on his laptop or desktop computer. A teen can be walking down the street, while downloading a movie into his hand-held smart phone. A government regime can manipulate elections by sending "misinformation" (the politically correct term for lies) into a nation's media. A hacker can be situated anyplace on, or even above, the planet, and infect the world's computer chips with a deadly virus.

Is it then unreasonable to believe that a chip inserted into a body could be controlled by a hacker? Could not a world ruler, in his mad ambition to control the planet, infect earth's inhabitants with lies through the chip? **Today, brains control the chip. Tomorrow, the chip will control brains.**

The ultimate goal of power-hungry tyrants is to control all mankind. This book reveals man's advances as he experiments in connecting inserted chips with the brain's neurons. It is shocking to learn how much is already accomplished, in man's quest to hack into the greatest "computer" on earth – the human brain. Is anyone naïve enough to believe that, in this day of blasphemous atheism, man would feed God's Word into the chip to encourage mankind to worship their Creator?

We do not know if the mark of the beast will involve an inserted chip. *But it may.* And if such a day comes, our desire is that you be warned.

The Chip, is just one more *piercing wail of a siren.*

THE CHIP

The Mark of the Beast

Can you imagine living in a world under a dictator who has the authority to take away your right to buy and sell? The Bible warns us that such a day is coming.

"And he causeth *(demands)* all, both small and great, rich and poor, free and bond, to receive a mark *in* their right hand, or *in* their foreheads: and that *no man might buy or sell*, save he that had the mark, or the name of the beast, or the number of his name. Here is wisdom. Let him that hath understanding count the number of the beast: for *it is the number of a man*; and his number is Six hundred three-score and six."
REVELATION 13:16-18

The coming dictator will shut anyone, who refuses to receive this mark, out of the economic system. But before we rush to receive it, we need to know God's warning that follows His prophecy. For the dictator will close the door to the coming economic system to anyone who dares to defy him. But, God will close the door to heaven to all who receive him and his mark!

God will shut people out of heaven, who do receive this mark!

Hear His warning: "... If any man worship the beast and his image, and *receive his mark in his forehead, or in his hand,* the same shall drink of the wine of the wrath of God, which is poured out without mixture into the cup of his indignation; and he shall be tormented with fire and brimstone in the presence of the holy angels, and in the presence of the Lamb; and the smoke of their torment ascendeth up for ever and ever: and they have no rest day nor night, who worship the beast and his image, and whosoever receiveth the mark of his name." REVELATION 14:9-11

We already live in a world that demands numbers for rights.

In the United States:

Our social security numbers give us **the right to work**.

Our drivers' license numbers give us **the right to drive**.

The Implanted Chip

The **Mark of the Beast** and **666** are phrases as old as the Bible. But "**the chip**" has meaning only to our modern computer generation.

Could the chip be what the Bible refers to as **the mark of the beast**?

What does the chip and its capabilities have to do with God, salvation, and man's eternal destiny? Can a nearly 2,000 year old Bible prophecy be pointing to an invention in our day?

If you will take the next few minutes to read this book, you will see that there are things going on today that will astound you. This book is an alert of men's plans. It is vital that you know them, for they involve you.

There is a sinister movement that has one wonderful goal - **to bring peace on earth**. Who does not long for a world without war? However, the Author of peace is the Prince of Peace - Jesus Christ. And men have no intention to involve Him in their quest for peace. There is only one way a so-called peace can be attained without Him. The man or government in leadership must have total control of **every** leader of **every** nation, **every** leader of **every** religion, **every** terrorist who harbors murder in his heart, **every** criminal... and ultimately **every single person** on the face of the earth. And that is where *you* come in. If you don't want your thoughts and your actions to be controlled by someone other than yourself, you need to be aware of plans that are already made for you. This is not science fiction...these are facts compiled from the ***Encyclopaedia Britannica***, reputable *science journals*, *Time magazine, CNN's Daily News, MSNBC's Technology News*, the ***BBC***, and some of the most respected computer geniuses of our day.

Please set aside the next few minutes to see what is planned for your future. Be prepared to be shocked!

Man's Dependency

Very few, if any, people are self-sufficient today. I personally don't know anyone who satisfies his craving for fried chicken by chopping off the neck of his bird, plucking its feathers, dissecting it into pieces with the knife he has tempered, rolling it in his home grown and ground flour, getting out the pan he has formed from the metal he has mined, placing it in the oil he has gleaned from his olive grove, and serving it on plates he has shaped at his potter's wheel, where it is placed on the table he has constructed from the tree in his forest. (By the time the chicken would be ready to eat, such a person would be too exhausted to chew!)

But I have heard more than once: "Let's have chicken tonight! Who's going to stop by the *Colonel's* and pick it up?"

We take our convenient way of living for granted. We are desperately in need of each other to provide us goods and services. People are a vital part of our daily lives, making, transporting, and selling us goods and then servicing them for us.

We live in a fast-paced society that is changing by the day. Our method of buying and selling is a prime example.

Cash transactions will soon be phased out. There are already "cash-free malls" and more than one country has nearly completed the transition from cash to microchips.

In days of old, goods and services were directly exchanged, without money, through a process called bartering. The old Trading Posts that dotted our country in its beginning days, were meeting places where hunters exchanged their furs, women exchanged their eggs, and farmers exchanged their crops.

Money was used to simplify this exchange. Money is nothing new. Historians tell us that money was invented over 4,000 years ago.

Aren't you glad some husband finally invented it? (We don't know for sure, but it was probably a husband who figured out that it was easier to fill a newly invented pocket with a few pieces of gold, silver, or copper, than to tote a few hundred eggs and several jugs of butter to the grocery store because his wife needed a bag of flour!)

Historians tell us that the largest currency that was used in the world is found on the Pacific Island of Yap, located southwest of

Guam. Sandstone slabs, shaped like millstones with holes in their middles, were used by aristocratic classes in rituals and were exchanged for goods. The largest slabs are taller than a man! (Can you imagine lugging one of them to the grocery store?)

No wonder nations decided that they could substitute paper money for precious metals and other commodities. Printing paper is easier than mining gold. In fact, as long as there are trees growing, there is no end to the amount of money that can be manufactured. At one time, paper money was a written promise, or note, to exchange for metal money on demand. Our nation's money was limited to our nation's supply of gold. A bill could be redeemed for gold, for its face value, at any commercial bank.

Then central banks took over the task of storing and redeeming gold for paper notes. In1934, the United States passed the **Gold Reserve Act**, and the **United States Treasury** took title to all gold coins, gold bullion, and gold certificates held by the central **Federal Reserve Banks.**

Today, there is much more paper in circulation than gold backing it up. Actually, there is nothing to guarantee that the paper you exchange today will be worth anything tomorrow. We can no longer exchange our paper for gold. President Richard Nixon severed the dollar from any connection to gold in 1971. Paper currency has replaced our gold reserves, and cheap metals have become substitutes for gold and silver.

Credit cards, debit cards, and smart cards are rapidly replacing the money we carry. A credit card is an instant loan by a financial lending institution. A clerk in Alabama swipes a credit card, and the buyer has instantly borrowed money from a bank in Nevada, Illinois, or California. Signatures become a promise to pay this loan, along with a specified amount of interest. This seems like a great method of exchange ... until the borrower is overloaded with debt. Then the lender, who was so kind, helpful, and courteous, turns into a vicious, snarling, threatening monster.

Few understood that a $3,000 balance on a credit card, that charges 18% interest, will require a $45 monthly payment for nearly 31 years! The borrower will pay over $13,300 in interest! (Note: When a borrower misses payments, the interest rate is often raised to 27.99%. This would mean that a $70 monthly payment would now be required. It would now take nearly 29 years to pay off, and the interest would cost the borrower over $21,000.)

Debit cards then made their debut. These eliminate the loans and resulting mountain of debt. With a swipe of one's card, an instant transaction occurs. Money is removed from the buyer's account and transferred into the seller's account. This is the simplest and speediest trade yet.

But, as always, currency continues to change with the times. Advertisements began enticing potential borrowers, announcing the newest form of exchange. One advertisement claimed: *The future is clear ... Smart Chip.* We are promised that the smart chip will give us a new level of convenience and security.

New credit and debit cards that have an embedded chip have already replaced the old. EMV chip technology is becoming the global standard for credit card and debit card payments. EMV derives its name from its original developers (**E**uropay, **M**asterCard, and **V**isa). As of this writing, there are approximately 2.4 billion EMV chip cards in circulation. They can currently be used in more than 130 countries, by means of nearly 37 million active terminals in the world.

Both buyers and sellers will soon realize just how smart this new chip will be.

The Smart Chip

What is this chip? How will it ultimately revolutionize - or shorten - our lives?

This miniature computer, or chip, has the capacity to hold our driver's license, cash, ATM card, credit card, insurance card, medical information, Social Security card, passport, telephone card, birth certificate, financial history, military records, marriage certificate, driving records, employment history, school records, club membership cards, library card, and any other cards that are stuffed in your wallet or purse. It will also contain whatever additional information man decides should be conveniently stored, so it can be accessed instantly.

The April, 1998 issue of **Time** magazine explained it like this: "A single electronic card may replace everything in your wallet, including your cash, your credit cards, your ATM card, your ID cards, your insurance ... and *your life*. **Future: One card, or one chip, with your life on it.**"

It has numerous advantages. The smart card will simplify travel. It will shorten time at the doctor's office, hospitals, and clinics. We will no longer be required to fill out long forms with our medical and insurance information. Doctors will no longer carry charts from room to room with patients' information. There will not be a stop at the cashier's office. All of one's medical history and insurance information will be gleaned from this one smart chip.

We will be assured that all this personal information will be locked safely into the chip, and will only be accessed by a digital reader, as needed. Doctors will have a unique code to access only our medical information; bankers will be able to access only our financial information; prospective employers only our job history, etc. (At least, that is how it is supposed to work.)

At the weigh stations for truckers along our nation's highways, the chip will insure a quick drive through. Makers of the new Idfocus electronic smart card allow truckers to weigh and refuel their vehicles without having to swipe a card through a slot or wave it past a sensor. They will pull up and transactions will be made instantly. The weight will be recorded through the chip.

The smart chip will not only be man's new electronic wallet, it will be his personal electronic file cabinet. Yet, it will be far more than that.

No longer will men have to carry slabs, beads, furs, or eggs to trade for goods. No longer will our wallets bulge with cards. The future is clear - one smart card will contain one tiny chip.

Cybercrime

Life for thieves and embezzlers is getting increasingly difficult. However, they are meeting the challenge by becoming smarter. Thieves have always devised ways to steal from those who work, as a way to avoid work themselves. The current crime wave is called cybercrime. Many have been victims of identity theft.

Cybercrime costs the global economy **up to $575 billion annually**, according to a 2015 report, with the U.S. taking a **$100 billion** hit, the largest of any country.

Today's currency experts are already perfecting their solution to this problem. They have decided that the best way to positively identify a person and thus eliminate theft, will be to move the chip from the card in the wallet into the person himself.

A smart card can be stolen. But can you imagine a society whose method of exchange is a smart chip in the hand or head? It would no doubt get immediate attention and arouse instant suspicion, if a thief tried to pass off someone else's head or hand as his own!

Changing all the currency of a nation costs a lot of money. Man has finally devised a method that he believes will be the ultimate currency. Men do not believe it will ever be surpassed by a better invention, nor will it need to be replaced. Computer scientists, universities, and companies are working around the clock to perfect this new *implantable chip*.

CNN's Daily News, MSNBC's Technology News, and the BBC have all introduced us to Professor Kevin Warwick, a Cybernetics Professor from the University of Reading in England. He has found a way to eliminate carrying the Smart Chip in his pocket. He had a 23-millimeter capsule, equipped with a computer chip and radio transmitter, surgically implanted into his biceps. Cybernetics is the study of humans and technology interacting. Who, more than a professor of Cybernetics, would decide to merge man with his machine? This chip enabled him to open doors, without lifting his finger, and flip on lights without touching a switch.

(Don't we live in a strange world today? Men buy the newest fad to eliminate movement, then fill their homes with exercise equipment so they can move!)

Back to the Professor ... When he walks
through the front door of his department at
work, the chip activates his computer, and
gives him a friendly greeting and his Email
status. His secretary can pinpoint his exact
whereabouts, at all times.

The professor explains why he had the chip
implanted. He claims that it was far more than
just an experiment. He wanted to demonstrate
the sinister side of the chip.

He explained, "There are positive sides and
negative sides - positive in helping people,
implanting prisoners or people we don't want
to get into our schools - negative are the big
brother issues - machines or computers
controlling humans. It gets very frightening.
If we look to the future, compared with what
this small chip contains now, in five or six
years' time, the amount of information and the
amount of processing capabilities will be
enormous."

He further stated that if their use became
widespread, we would never enjoy any privacy
and could be followed and identified wherever
we went. The article in **BBC** adds: "Criminal
offenders and even babies can already be
tracked using electronic tagging devices
attached to their body. The next step could be

to implant silicon chips in the place of the tags."

This was astounding news just a few years ago. Now we are accustomed to implanting chips into our pets. Biologists track fish, birds, and animals. Some parents implant chips into their children. GPS Smart Soles feature shoe sole inserts that contain a miniature chip. The inserts are then placed into the shoes of those with memory impairment, in order to monitor their location. Embedded chips are showing up everywhere!

Why would this English Cybernetics Professor be so concerned about the implanted chip, that he went to the extreme of having one implanted into himself? Professor Warwick knows how far man has progressed in his study of Cybernetics. We need to know too, for it involves our future.

How Close Are We?

Chief Justice John Roberts appeared before a senate confirmation hearing in September, 2005. A Senator from Delaware spoke these words to Judge Roberts during the hearing: "There are those who would slash the power of our national government, fragmenting it among the states in a new reading of the 10th and 11th amendment. Judge, I don't believe in a constitution where individuals could for very long have accomplished what we did had we read it in such a narrow way. Our constitutional journey did not stop with women being barred from being lawyers, with 10-year-olds working in coal mines. Our constitutional journey did not stop then and it must not stop now, Judge. And we'll be faced with equally consequential decisions in the 21st century. **Can a microscopic tag be implanted in a person's body to track his every movement? There's actual discussion about that. You will rule on that - mark my words - before your tenure is over."**

The senator who spoke these words was Joe Biden, who became the Vice President of the United States in January, 2009.

Leaders in high places know exactly where government control is heading. And they know that the microscopic tag will be part of that control. A special article by Ray Kurzweil to MSNBC includes this warning: "There will not be a clear distinction between human and machine in the 21st century. First of all, we will be putting computers - neural implants - directly into our brains. We've already started down this path. Scientists recently placed a chip in the brain of a paralyzed individual who can now control his environment directly from his brain. In the 2020s, neural implants will not be just for disabled people. Most of us will have neural implants to improve our sensory experiences, perception, memory, and logical thinking. These implants will also plug us in directly to the World Wide Web. Virtual reality will be as realistic, detailed, and *subtle* as real reality." (It amazes us that Mr. Kurzweil used the word subtle. It is the same word used to describe the serpent, whose intention was to lure Eve into deception. **Subtle** (or subtil) means *sly; deceitful; cunning; treacherous*.)

Another article submitted to MSNBC by Glenn McGee, Ph.D., is titled **"The Merging of Man and Machine."**

McGee wrote: "Human machine integration isn't just fiction anymore. Teams at MIT, Xerox, and elsewhere are racing to connect you very closely to your cell phone and television."

Revealing Excerpts From Articles

Steve Johnson McClatchy: Mobile Press Register; January, 2014:

"It is likely the world in the not-so-distant future will be increasingly populated by computerized people like Amal Graafstra. The 37-year-old doesn't need a key or password to get into his car, home, or computer. He's programmed them to unlock at the mere wave of his hands, which are implanted with radio frequency identification tags. The rice-size gadgets work so well, the Seattle resident says, he's sold similar ones to more than 500 customers through his company, *Dangerous Things*.

"The move to outfit people with electronic devices that can be swallowed, implanted in their bodies, or attached to their skin via 'smart tattoos' could revolutionize health care and change the way people interact with devices — and one another.

Critics call the trend intrusive, even sacrilegious. But others say it ultimately will make life better for everybody. Some researchers and executives envision a day when devices placed in people will enable them to control computers, prosthetic devices, and many other things solely with their thoughts. 'In the next 10 to 20 years, we will see rapid development in bioengineered and man-machine interfaces,' predicted Graafstra, who wrote a book about the technology, adding that the trend is going to 'push the boundaries of what it means to be human.'"

Brainstorm

In a patent application made public in November, 2013, Google's Motorola Mobility branch proposed an "electronic skin tattoo" for the throat, with a built-in microphone, battery, and wireless transceiver that would let someone operate other devices via voice commands. When asked, Google said it often seeks patents on employee brainstorms and that, while "some of those ideas later mature into real products or services, some don't." But Google CEO ,Larry Page, apparently is intrigued with enhancing people electronically.

A 2011 book about the Mountain View, California search giant quoted him saying, "Eventually you'll have an implant, where if you think about a fact, it will just tell you the answer."

Similar notions are under study by others, including University of California - Berkeley researchers. In a scholarly paper published in July, 2013, they proposed implanting people's brains with thousands of tiny sensors they called "neural dust."

The idea initially is to have the little circuits gather detailed data on brain functions.

"But eventually," lead researcher, Dongjin Seo, said, "the electronic swarms may prove useful for controlling devices via thought, or stimulating malfunctioning brain regions to restore limb motor control for paralyzed patients."

After learning about a Cincinnati video surveillance firm that required employees to have a chip inserted in them, California state Senator, Joe Simitian, introduced a bill that became law in 2008, forbidding anyone in this state from making similar demands.

Two years later, when the Virginia House of Delegates passed a similar measure, some of the lawmakers (citing biblical references about the Antichrist) denounced implanted chips as "the mark of the beast."

Baby Steps

Intel futurist, Brian David Johnson, believes that the public initially will be more amenable to smart tattoos than computerized pills or gadgets inserted into them, because "something on your skin, that's a baby step" compared to a swallowed or surgically implanted device.

One tattoo being developed by MC10 of Cambridge, Massachusetts, would temporarily attach to the skin like an adhesive bandage and wirelessly transmit the wearer's vital signs to a phone or other device. The company, which has a contract for a military version, plans to introduce one next year for consumers, according to MC10 official, Barry Ives Jr., who touted its use for "athletes, expectant and new moms, and the elderly."

In a recent patent application, Finnish phone-maker, Nokia, proposed a tattoo that would vibrate when the person gets a phone call, or serve as a mobile-device password and attach to the skin with "ferromagnetic powder."

Among the critical issues to be resolved, is how to keep implanted devices updated with the latest software, maintain their battery power, and shield them from hackers. But Eric Dishman, who heads Intel's health care innovation team, predicts that the gadgets, particularly those providing health benefits, will become common someday.

"There's going to be an ecosystem of things on and in the body," he predicted, adding, this is the ultimate in personalized medicine."

Motorola is producing microchips for the Mondex Smartcard, and has already developed several human implantable biochips.

A report from ABC News says: "Computer chips under one's skin, phone devices that turn on appliances, and phone numbers given out at birth may be future trends. Each person may be assigned a phone number or a communications number at birth that will stay with him for life. It may be technologically possible in the future to embed a computer chip under one's skin as a link to communications networks and one another, though society may be slow to embrace such advances.

'A phone connected to the house is something quaint that we'll tell our children about. A phone number per dwelling is an antique idea,' said Pat Morreale, an associate professor of computer science at the Stevens Institute in New Jersey and director of the Advances Telecommunications Institute. 'A phone number per person is the future.'"

What better way for society to assign every person their personal number, than to introduce a new telephone numbering system?

Who among us wants to be shut out of the telephone system? The telephone system itself will be integrated with implanted chips!

An article that was written over ten years ago, introduced us to the first business that implanted chips into its clients.

"The Baja Beach Club in Barcelona, Spain, has given their VIP patrons easy access to their club. They have implanted them with a syringe-injected microchip. VIPs no longer have to wait in lines for identification, but pass right by a 'reader' that recognizes their identity, credit balance, and even opens doors to exclusive areas of the club for them. They can buy drinks and food with a wave of their hand. In the popular club, which boasts a dance floor that can accommodate 3,000, streamlined services and convenience matter to

VIP customers who are thrilled with their implants.

"Baja Beach Clubs International is the first firm to employ the VeriPay System, developed by Applied Digital's VeriChip Corporation (now called The PositiveID Corporation) and announced at an international conference in Paris last year. The company praises this application of the chip implant as an advance over credit cards and smart cards, which are subject to thefts resulting in identity fraud. Similar to pet identification chips, the VeriChip is a radio frequency, syringe-injectable identification microchip that can be read from a few feet away by either a hand-held scanner or by the implantee walking through a 'portal' scanner. Information can be wirelessly written to the chip, which contains a unique 10-digit identification number. Last year, Art Kranzley, senior vice president at Master-Card, speculated on possible future electronic payment media. 'Ultimately, it could be embedded in anything - someday, maybe even under the skin.' The nightclub director calls the chip implant the wave of the future. He says, 'I know many people who want to be implanted. Actually, almost everybody has piercings, tattoos, or silicone.'

The objective of this technology at the club is to bring an ID system to a global level that will destroy the need to carry ID documents and credit cards."

The CEO of VeriChip, Dr. Keith Bolton, said the company's goal was to market the VeriChip as a global implantable identification system. They expect a law that would force all gun owners to be required to have a microchip implanted in their hand to be able to own a gun - a potential universal method of gun control. The Italian government is currently preparing to implant its government workers.

VeriChip has retained the services of Stanley L. Reid, a longtime technology industry executive and former congressional aide, with extensive experience and wide contacts in Washington, D.C. Since 1996, Mr. Reid has served as president of Strategic Sciences, a Washington, D.C. area consulting firm that specializes in marketing advanced technologies to the federal government. Mr. Reid has particular expertise in selling new, introductory technologies to government agencies, including the Departments of Defense, Energy, and State, as well as the agencies that have been incorporated into the

Department of Homeland Security. The Company has been actively developing applications for VeriChip in which VeriChip could be used to control authorized access to government installations and private-sector buildings, nuclear power plants, national research laboratories, and sensitive transportation resources including airports and seaports.

As Visa advertised, **"The future is clear - smart chip."**

If VeriChip has its way, government officials will have to be first implanted with a chip, before being able to enter their place of work. In other words, only men who have the chip will be allowed to work in our sensitive government areas!

In this day of terrorist threats, we can understand why the chip sounds good to man and governments. But read on! For the chip is more than just a new convenience for mankind. It has a dark side that is not being revealed to the unsuspecting public.

Mind Control

Researchers at the University of California have been studying ways of simulating brain functions, through the use of synthetic microchips. Their aim is to have the implanted microchip eventually become a real and integrated part of the brain. It is theorized that the brain actually may start to grow cells in and around the chip, and will eventually accept the chip as part of itself.

In an experiment by an American neuro-physiologist, an electronic receiver was implanted into a bull's brain. The scientist stood in a bull ring with the bull as it charged toward him. Before being bludgeoned by the charging bull, the scientist pressed a button in his remote control that sent a signal to the bull's brain and successfully made him stop in his tracks.

You may want to read that last paragraph again.

The violent criminal will be subdued, just as the bull was stopped short of charging the scientist. This coming chip will go far beyond becoming simply our "electronic purse" and "electronic files"!

The chip in this raging bull did not just *give* a message from the inside out! It *received* a message ... from the outside in! The bull was ***programmed, through the implanted chip!***

If this seems like science "fiction" to you, read the following excerpt from ***Special Report on Cyberspace*** by Robert Everett-Green in the 1996 Encyclopaedia Britannica, Inc. Book of the Year: Events of 1995 (Page 159): "The most intriguing aspect of cyberspace, however, may have more to do with the evolving relationship of humankind with its technologies. At the root of Gibson's notion of computer-simulated worlds and electronically assisted experience is the prospect of a meeting of machine and human at a near-organic level. Some commentators have spoken of a coming 'bionic convergence' through which **we may all someday be fitted with *computer implants that shunt messages directly to and from our brains*** and that may have the capacity to stimulate electronically our creativity or our response to pleasure."

This article clearly states that messages will not only be directed *from* our brains through the chip . . . but *to* them *through* the chip!

CNN quotes Professor Warwick: "If successful, the computer could send a signal directly into a person's nervous system. I think there are enormous possibilities as far as electronic medicine is concerned. Ideally, the implant will also allow **the computer to manipulate a person's emotions**. The goal there is to create an electronic cure for depression. If we can change a person's emotions electronically, record a time when they're happy, and then when they're sad, we can send in electronic signals that cheer them up." CNN went on to say that Professor Warwick believes that this is the next step in human evolution.

Do you want someone implanting messages directly into your brain, bypassing your ability to filter them?

From **Natural News**: "New Brain Implants are so microscopic, you won't even know that you've been implanted. The cult of science is trying to amalgamate humanity with machine. Its latest endeavor has taken the form of an emerging brain implant technology that would render humans part flesh, part computer. **Government-funded implantable brain chips will read (and) control people's thoughts**."

As Ritalin controls our children; psychotic drugs control the patients in our mental institutions; brain-numbing drugs bring peace to residents of our nursing homes; pain-killers deaden hospitalized minds and bodies; and pills sedate our prison populations; the chip will finally go a step beyond. It will control the thoughts of the entire human race. The problem is: who will control the chip that controls mankind?

Today, we hear from our politicians and nation's leaders that we must invest more money into mental health, as a means of reducing mass shootings, etc. Do they need to finance more drugs; more psychiatrists and counsellors; or more insane asylums?

Or could they need added funds to finance implantable brain chips?

Man's plans are not hidden. Read the following article from *The Sovereign Health Group of California*, published on June 4, 2014, under the category of mental health.

MILITARY FUNDS IMPLANTABLE BRAIN CHIP RESEARCH TO TREAT MENTAL ILLNESSES

"Defense Advanced Research Projects Agency (DARPA), the research arm of the **United States Department of Defense**, is funding two major research initiatives to *create implantable electronic devices* to monitor and treat seven different *psychiatric disorders*, including addiction, anxiety, depression, post-traumatic stress disorder (PTSD), and chronic pain.

"The **DARPA SUBNETS** (*Systems-Based Neurotechnology for Emerging Therapies*) program has committed $12 million (plus an additional $26 million, if performance benchmarks are met) to the projects, which will be led by research teams at the **University of California**, San Francisco (UCSF), and Boston's **Massachusetts General Hospital**. The project will also involve researchers, physicians, and engineers at the **University of California** at Berkeley, **Cornell University** at Ithaca, New York, and **New York University**. The research projects fall under President

Obama's **BRAIN** *(Brain Research through Advancing Innovative Neurotechnologies)* **Initiative**, launched in April, 2013. The DARPA funded research project will examine the interaction of the parts of the brain in mental illnesses in a new way... *implants may cause the brain to remodel itself and alleviate symptoms of mental health disorders.*

"Implantable Devices: New miniature implantable devices will be designed and *implanted in the brain* to gain information about neural circuits responsible for psychiatric disorders. These devices, known as brain-machine interfaces (BMIs), will record neural activity in detail. This recorded information will be the foundation for development of effective neural stimulation therapies such as the **therapeutic brain chips**, which can be used *in a guided and precise manner to correct abnormal activity in the human brain.*

"It is hoped that by the use of novel electrical stimulation techniques, **the brain would unlearn** the disrupted signaling patterns that are regarded as the basis of *mental diseases.*

"After the identification of aberrant brain signaling pathways associated with symptoms of anxiety and depression, researchers hope to develop *devices for providing precise and effective brain stimulation to treat such symptoms* ... The concept is that *electronic stimulation will help guide the brain to remodel itself to strengthen alternative neural circuits*. The newly strengthened alternative neural circuits, developed by the use of deep brain stimulation, will bypass the signals associated with mental illnesses, eliminating symptoms. More than $42 billion dollars (1/3 of U.S. spending on mental illness), goes toward the treatment of anxiety disorders, affecting 40 million adult Americans."

From a CBS News transcript, May 27, 2014: DARPA PROGRAM TO DEVELOP BRAIN IMPLANTS FOR MENTAL DISORDERS

"The **Defense Advanced Research Projects Agency** has announced plans for a cutting-edge technology-based research program to *develop a tiny, implanted chip in the skull to* *treat psychiatric disorders such as anxiety, PTSD, and major depression*. The researchers expect to ultimately use the project results to develop potential therapies aimed at 'teaching' the brain to 'unlearn' the detrimental patterns that underlie such disorders."

From The Chicago Tribune:
Brain Power

"The day is coming when to learn French or read the classics, you'll just hook up a computer to the chip inside your head. Are we ready for that?"

USA Today, March 27, 2014:
IMPLANTABLE TECHNOLOGY WILL GET UNDER OUR SKIN

"Implantable, also referred to as 'embeddable,' technology refers to a class of objects that can be inserted directly into the human body to **modify, enhance, or heal** ... *We will just gently start integrating these things into our bodies.*"

Headline in SCIENCE, September 18, 2014 Issue:

"TINY IMPLANTS COULD GIVE HUMANS SELF-HEALING SUPERPOWERS"

We have now learned that the designers of these implantable chips tell us that they will be our personal identification; track us through GPS; contain our medical records and history; enable us to make financial transactions; and even give us both mental and physical health! Few would refuse the offer to not only be able to buy and sell in tomorrow's emerging new world, but to enjoy health! Today's scientists are programming the chips to retrain the brain to heal the body! Multitudes will rush to receive it!

Transhumanism

There is a widespread effort today to artificially evolve humans into a higher state through transhumanism. Transhumanism works toward "transforming the human condition, by developing and creating widely available sophisticated technologies to *greatly enhance human intellectual, physical, and psychological capacities*."

We have now learned that super intelligence has been added into the wonders of the chip!

These incredible brain implants will:

- eliminate identity theft;
- heal the mentally ill;
- replace depression with happiness;
- cause our brains to heal our bodies;
- keep track of our children, the elderly, and our soldiers;
- eliminate money laundering;
- hamper the illegal drug trade;
- stop tax fraud;

- identify victims of natural or man-made disasters;
- solve the illegal immigration problem;
- rid our minds of thoughts and memories that cause us to be sad;
- make us smarter; and
- **give us the right to buy and sell.**

Quantum Computers

There is a new language in today's world. Scientists are now researching the wonders of the D-Wave of quantum computing. Today's scientists claim that by harvesting the "parallel worlds", we will be able to tap into limitless resources of wisdom to solve our world's problems. Lest you think this is too far out, consider the fact that the leaders of this project are **NASA** and **Google.** NASA's leading scientists tell us that parallel worlds will sound strange to us.

However, the concept should not sound strange to the Bible student. We know that there is a "**parallel world**". Jesus referred to the prince of the world. He said: "… the prince of this world cometh, and hath nothing in me." (John 14:30) There was no darkness in Jesus Christ for the devil to appeal to. He was – and is - pure Light.

Jesus delivered people that this dark world had held in captivity. This kingdom was inhabited by devils, fallen angels, and unclean spirits. Jesus confronted it with power. He cast a legion of devils out of one man. The unseen devils of the parallel world ran into a herd of swine. The 2,000 pigs ran violently down a steep hill and drowned themselves in the sea. Before His ascension to heaven, Jesus gave His followers power to battle this parallel world and to conquer it. He said: "Behold, I give unto you power to tread on serpents and scorpions, and over all the power of the enemy ..." (LUKE 10:19)

We know that this kingdom of darkness would love to respond to men's invitation to give them wisdom to solve all of earth's problems. Since the day that Eve was lured into it by Satan's offer to make her wise if she would only disobey God, humanity has been drawn into this "parallel world". The Bible strictly forbids entry into it - yet the occult world, with its witches, wizards, astrologers, sorcerers, fortune tellers, soothsayers, magicians, mediums (the Bible describes these as people with familiar spirits), enchanters, and charmers, continues to draw victims into its darkness.

Its bait is to become smarter, by gaining superior intelligence and wisdom. The serpent is now drawing NASA into its depths of wickedness, by means of a quantum computer

D-2 that will give mankind (in their own scientists' words), "by harvesting the 'parallel worlds', the ability to tap into limitless resources of wisdom to solve our world's problems."

Whether it is a fortune teller in a dark alley, calling her prey to learn their future from her, or it is a multi-million dollar computer owned by NASA, the result is the same, when men seek knowledge and wisdom from a source other than God and His Word.

Listen to these statements about the end-day beasts, taken from the 13th chapter of Revelation: "And **the dragon gave him his power**, and his seat, and great authority." (VERSE 2)

"And they worshipped **the dragon, which gave power unto the beast**." (VERSE 4)

"He spake as **a dragon**." (VERSE 11)

Who is this dragon?

Revelation 12:9 identifies him: "And the great dragon was cast out, that old serpent, called the Devil, and Satan, which deceiveth the whole world: he was cast out into the earth, and his angels were cast out with him."

The dragon is none other than the old serpent in the Garden of Eden, who promised Eve wisdom and godhood, if she would rebel against her Creator! He is promising men the same things today.

The beasts that are coming will have no rest until they have total global control. The leading men of these new movements define their goal as "Global Governance". They are not hiding their plans. We can hear this term in many of their speeches. The following is the stated mission of the Global Governance Institute:

"The Global Governance Institute (GGI) is an independent, non-profit think tank based in Brussels. GGI brings together senior policy-makers, scholars, and practitioners from the world's leading institutions in order to devise, strengthen, and improve forward-looking approaches to **global governance**."

This statement was made, on April 2, 2013, by President Obama, as he announced the launch of the **BRAIN** (**B**rain **R**esearch through **A**dvancing **I**nnovative **N**eurotechnologies)

Initiative: "We have a chance to improve the lives of not just millions, but billions of people on this planet through the research that's done in this BRAIN Initiative alone."

You may recognize some corporations, names, and universities that have aligned with and are financially supporting the **BRAIN Initiative**:

- **University of Pittsburgh** - more than $45 million

- **The Simons Foundation** - $62 million

- **The Carnegie Mellon University** - $40 million

- **University of Texas System** - $20 million

- **University of California**, Berkeley and Carl Zeiss Microscopy - $12 million

- **University of Utah** - $10 million

- **Boston University** - $140 million

- **U.S. Photonics Industry** Leaders - $30 million

- **General Electric** - a $60 million open innovation challenge

- **Google** engineers

- **FDA**

- **Howard Hughes Medical Institutes**
  Janelia Research Campus - over $70
  million

- **IARPA** (the Intelligence Advanced
  Research Projects Activity within the
  Office of the Director of National
  Intelligence

- **The Pacific Northwest Neuroscience
  Neighborhood**

  ... and the list of sponsors, who
  contribute both their research and their
  financial support, not only continues,
  but is growing.

Killing to Advance Science

From *PC Magazine,* September 4, 2001 issue, by Peter Schwartz (founder of the **Global Business Network,** and associated with DARPA. Schwartz scours the globe in search of research initiatives that might produce major upheavals in the future):

"I've been asked to set my sights 20 or 30 years out," he said, "to the place where the line between science and science fiction gets blurry. **Within 20 or 30 years, technicians might endow a so-so brain with the quality of genius.** Science and technology will only exacerbate the conflict between the secular and the sacred. **The biggest political challenge in this new century is the conflict between the secular and the sacred - between secular societies and religious societies.** Cloning, life extension, genetic manipulation, super intelligence, sentient robots ... touches on fundamental issues of human identity. What is a human? Are we God-endowed or just chemicals? If I succeed in growing a cell out of chemicals, what does that say about God?

If I can manufacture an iris or something even more beautiful, what does that say about God? These are the sorts of questions we'll confront. The issues will be profound. **And the conflicts will be life-and-death. In the next few decades, I do believe people will kill each other in large numbers as a direct result of the advancement of science."**

Why Is God Against This New Currency?

Why would God get involved in the currency man uses? What difference should it make to Him? God never objected when men used gold, furs, beads, silver, the dollar, euro, peso, or yen. What would cause Him to get angry over the new chip? Is He not the Creator, who gave man dominion over all the earth, according to the Genesis account? **Dominion** means that man has *authority, control, rule, ownership, possession*.

Jesus did not criticize the Roman currency system when He was handed a penny with Caesar's picture on it, even though Caesar claimed to be the god of the world. You may remember the story. Jesus was teaching one day when someone asked: "Is it lawful to give tribute *(taxes)* to Caesar, or not?"

Jesus answered, "Bring me a penny, that I may see it." Looking at the penny, He then asked them "Whose is this image and superscription?"

And they said unto him, "Caesar's."

And Jesus answering said unto them, "Render to Caesar the things that are Caesar's, and to God the things that are God's." MARK 12:14-17

Jesus did not refuse to touch the penny and declare it wicked, because it held the picture of a ruthless dictator of a corrupt nation. He simply said, roughly translated, "Take this penny and pay your taxes! Caesar wants pennies - so give him pennies!"

God has never seemed to care what system man uses to buy and sell. He has **never** intervened or pronounced judgment on man's method of currency! But He has sentenced any man, woman, teenager, or child to hell if he or she receives this chip.

Why? Is 6 an evil number? There are 66 books in the Bible.

Genesis 46:26 tells us: "All the souls that came with Jacob into Egypt, which came out of his loins, besides Jacob's sons' wives, all the souls were threescore and six (66)."

Solomon received 666 talents of gold yearly. God created man on the 6th day, and said that His creation was very good! God did not hesitate to use the number 6. He did not care what man exchanged as currency ... even when it had Caesar's picture on it!

So why will men go to hell if they receive this final currency? Why is this bartering system so evil that hell itself is the future for everyone who receives it? The problem is that this new implanted chip is not just a new currency system.

Buying and selling is just the bait that is used to entrap man into a new structure of total mind control and ultimate population control! The men leading the world will send messages directly into man's brain through the implanted chip!

God has not cared what currency we use. However, God has ***always*** cared about who we worship! He issued this commandment, in Exodus 34:14: "For **thou shalt worship no other god**: for the LORD, whose name is Jealous is a jealous God."

The problem is that the world's final currency is much more than just a modern way of bartering. **The new system of exchange will determine who man worships**. This new currency is referred to as the "mark of the beast".

Everyone who receives it will worship the beast, instead of God. The final currency will involve total mind and population control.

While we have been going about our daily business of work, eating, playing, and sleeping, scientists have been at work studying the brain. They have discovered that the brain has the ability to form new connections between neurons. They have identified the electrical signals. They have measured the size of the voltages associated with these signals. They know that the voltages travel 200 miles an hour. They know how often the neurons fire. They know the different patterns of electrical firing activity. They know what transmission chemicals are needed to form connections between neurons.

Why do you think they are studying all this? The answer is simple. They are perfecting a way to send messages directly to the brain through the implanted chip. Will they succeed? God said they would. ***"All that dwell upon the earth shall worship him***, whose names are not written in the book of life of the Lamb slain from the foundation of the world." REVELATION 13:8

What do you think could cause the entire world to reject Mohammed, Buddha, Confucius, and all the other various men that are revered as gods, and direct their worship to one man? People don't agree! Juries seldom agree on verdicts, and thus spend hours, days, and even weeks trying to hash out their differences. Voters don't agree on politicians. Senators don't agree. Congressmen don't agree. Yet - the end-day world will be under the world leader's control - and every single one (with the exception of the children of God, whose names are written in the Lamb's book of life) will not only agree - but will worship just one man. And that's *when*, and that's *why* God will intervene.

The world consists of men with varied beliefs, preferences, goals, and personalities. How could the entire world center its worship on one man? The only answer is worldwide mind control. The implant into human brains will accomplish what would otherwise be impossible.

Imaging

We consistently find the word, **imaging**, in man's quest to build a better world, by building new and improved humans. They view their "improvement" of humans as man's next step in evolution.

Imaging ... Virtual reality could literally place the antichrist in every place of the globe, in front of every man, woman, and child.

(**Note:** we also find the word, *"image"*, ten times in the book of Revelation. Each time, it is associated with the beast. And the beast is empowered by the dragon, or Satan, who "deceiveth the whole world.") SEE REVELATION 12:9

The final currency system of man will be placed **in** the right hand or **in** the forehead.

Buying and selling is just the bait.

Total mind control is the result.

Jesus said, in Luke 21:35, that it would come **as a snare** on *all them that dwell on the face of the whole earth*. A snare is a **web.** A web is a network of fine threads, constructed by a spider, used to catch its prey. One of the definitions of a net is a system or procedure for catching or entrapping someone.

It is interesting that billions of computers are linked together today, through the World Wide **WEB** and the inter**NET**.

We do not know exactly what happened in the days before the flood.

Genesis 6:4-5 tells us: "There were giants in the earth in those days; and also after that, when the sons of God came in unto the daughters of men, and they bare children to them, the same became mighty men which were of old, men of renown. And God saw that the wickedness of man was great in the earth, and that every imagination of the thoughts of his heart was only evil continually."

So the flood came. Everyone drowned but Noah and his family. Noah alone found grace, in the eyes of the Lord.

Today, man again is tampering with the human race. His current goal is to merge inferior men with superior machines. And once again, destruction will follow. God will destroy every single person who has the mark of the beast, because his thoughts, programmed by the devil himself, will be continually evil.

Mankind will be void of a conscience. He will no longer have any sense of morality - of right and wrong. Only those, who have received God's only begotten Son, Jesus Christ, and His Gift of grace, will survive the coming destruction.

Revelation 13:8 states clearly: "And **all that dwell upon the earth shall worship him,** *whose names are not written in the book of life of the Lamb slain from the foundation of the world.*"

We remind you that NASA and Google are cooperating together, in their quest to harvest wisdom from "parallel worlds" through their quantum computer, D-2.

The man who will control the chip will be controlled by the devil!

"... and the dragon gave him his power, and his seat, and great authority ... and all the world wondered after the beast. And ***they worshipped the dragon which gave power unto the beast.***" FROM REVELATION 13:2-4

Again, we remind you of the identity of the dragon that empowers the last world dictator.

"And the great dragon was cast out, **that old serpent**, called the Devil, and Satan, which deceiveth the whole world." REVELATION 12:9

This "beast" gets his power from the devil! No wonder he "opened his mouth in blasphemy against God, to blaspheme his name, and his tabernacle, and them that dwell in heaven." No wonder "it was given unto him to make war with the saints..." (SEE REVELATION 13:6-7.)

This tiny chip will ultimately turn the population of the entire world, with the exception of true followers of Jesus Christ, into devil worshipers!

And this is why God will once again step down to the scene.

He intervened before, when the thoughts of men's minds were continually evil. He salvaged Noah and his family, and wiped out the rest of the human race. God is concerned about the thoughts of men!

Have you ever wondered if Jesus is *ever really* coming back? If the promise of His return is true, why hasn't He yet returned to take control of this mess that men have made of the world?

Peter wrote that many people in our day would ridicule anyone who still believes the promise Jesus made that He would return.

"There shall come in the last days scoffers, walking after their own lusts, and saying, Where is the promise of his coming?"
II PETER 3:3-4

A few verses later, Peter explained, "The Lord is not slack concerning his promise, as some men count slackness; but is longsuffering to usward, *not willing that any should perish, but that all should come to repentance*." II PETER 3:8

Now think about the future, under the new implanted chip system. The world will finally be controlled. The New Age will have arrived. All, but a few real followers of Jesus, will direct their worship to one devil possessed man. The entire world will have taken the bait and will be subdued through mind control. All people - *everyone - with the exception of born again saints* - will have been implanted with the chip. When the chips have been inserted and minds are programmed to worship Satan's leader, mankind then will have already received their final sentence of eternal hell.

The Bible says that this ruling Beast has power "… over *all kindreds, and tongues, and nations*. And *all that dwell upon the earth shall worship him,* whose names are not written in the book of life of the Lamb slain from the foundation of the world." REVELATION 13:7-8

All simply means … *all.*

Jesus will no longer need to wait for that one last soul to repent. There will be no one left on earth who will be able to repent and come to Christ for salvation.

God's longsuffering never runs out.

But man's opportunity to receive God's longsuffering will run out.

It will be at this time that Jesus will come. He will no longer be waiting for one more person to repent of his sins, be cleansed by His redeeming blood, and be saved. There will be no one left who can turn to Christ. That's when Jesus will return. He will rid our world once and for all of devil worshipers. Jesus will then rule over the people who chose to worship God.

The prophet, Daniel, wrote his vision of these latter days. "I beheld, and **the same horn made**

war with the saints, and prevailed against them; <u>until</u> the Ancient of days came, and judgment was given to the saints of the most High; and the time came that the saints possessed the kingdom." DANIEL 7:21-22

Temptation

Let us look again at this chip implant. If this is the world's last currency, what will followers of Jesus Christ do when there is no other way to buy and sell?

It is hard to even begin to imagine the temptation that will face the Christians to receive this mark. Satan will tempt the body of Christ *(true followers of Jesus Christ)*, just as he tempted Jesus when He walked the earth nearly 2,000 years ago.

Matthew 4:1-10 tells us about Christ's temptation. "Then was Jesus led up of the Spirit into the wilderness *to be tempted of the devil."*

Jesus was victorious over the first two temptations.

Then "… the devil taketh him up into an exceeding high mountain, and showeth him all the kingdoms of the world, and the glory of them; and saith unto him, *All these things will I give thee, if thou wilt fall down and worship me."*

The devil will come to the end-day body of Christ and this will be his offer: ***"Do you want to buy and sell? Do you want your piece of the world? Just take the mark. Worship me!"***

Every single true follower of Jesus Christ will answer the devil just as our Lord did: "Then saith Jesus unto him, Get thee hence, Satan: for it is written, ***Thou shalt worship the Lord thy God, and him only shalt thou serve."***

Only **JESUS** could overcome the temptation of the devil.

Only the body of Christ, whose members are empowered by their indwelling Lord, not an implanted chip, will overcome the temptation of the devil in the days ahead.

The offers *(the devil's bait)* are already arriving in our mail boxes. On the envelope of the most recent one we received is:

"THE FUTURE IS CLEAR: SMART CHIP"

This is the message inside:

"AS THE FUTURE CHANGES, SO WILL THE CAPABILITIES OF YOUR SMART CHIP."

What Will You Do?

What will your choice be? Will you choose to accept the implanted chip?

Or will you choose to opt out of the right to buy and the right to sell?

Some may answer that their choice will be made when that time comes.

It will be too late then.

Many choices have to be made beforehand. This is one.

The teenager has a choice to accept or refuse a ride home with the drunken driver. She chooses to get into the car. When the car is careening out of control toward another vehicle across the median, she has no choice. Her choice was already made. The accident is inevitable, and she has nothing to say about it. The echo of her scream indicates that she made the wrong choice.

The eighteen year old has chosen to spend his evening with the wrong crowd. It wasn't his idea to join in the armed robbery and murder. In fact, he was against it. But he was there. His bad choice robbed him of several years of choices. It was the judge, who told him where he would live. The prison warden chose what and when he would eat, what he would wear, when he would go to bed, and what time he would get up. He could not even choose his roommates.

The choice is made to drown problems in alcohol. No drunkard chooses to die a premature death from the resulting cirrhosis of the liver. That fate was determined by his earlier choice to drink.

A pilot friend of ours chose to ignore the warnings of adverse weather. It was only a short trip home, and he chose to fly. He had no choice a few minutes later, as his plane plummeted to the ground. The final decision of his life had been made earlier. He made the wrong choice.

So it is with the chip. Whether or not you receive it, is predetermined by your earlier choice. If your name has not been penned in the Lamb's book of Life, you will receive the mark.

"... power was given him over *all kindreds, and tongues, and nations*. And *all that dwell upon the earth shall worship him*, whose names are not written in the book of life of the Lamb slain from the foundation of the world." REVELATION 13:7-8

The choice that **needs to be made now** is to receive Jesus Christ as your Savior and Lord.

II Corinthians 6:2 tells us when the choice must be made. "... *now* is the accepted time; behold, *now* is the day of salvation.

"Oh, I'm already a Christian," many Americans will answer. And for many Americans, their choice was an easy one. They were told that they only had to say a few words, and their eternal home in heaven was guaranteed. Their salvation was determined by what they said – not what Christ did.

Do you want to gain heaven? Say a prayer. A few words, a minute or two out of their day, and life continued, unchanged.

But is that all that there is to our choice?

What does it *really* mean to make Jesus our Savior?

The Bible says: "Therefore *if any man be in Christ*, he is a new creature: old things are passed away; behold, all things are become new." II CORINTHIANS 5:17

And what does it *really* mean to make Jesus our Lord?

"Not every one that *saith* unto me, Lord, Lord, shall enter into the kingdom of heaven; but he that *doeth* the will of my Father which is in heaven. And why call ye me, Lord, Lord, and do not the things which I say?"
MATTHEW 7:21 & LUKE 6:46

What does *Lord* mean? **Lord** means *Master; absolute Ruler; Owner*. Jesus has bought His followers. The price He paid was His blood.

The Bible says, "What? know ye not that your body is the temple of the Holy Ghost which is in you, which ye have of God, and *ye are not your own?* For *ye are bought with a price*: therefore glorify God in your body, and in your spirit, which are God's."
I CORINTHIANS 6:19-20

Acts 20:28 speaks of the "... church of God, which he hath purchased with his own blood."

What does **Lord** mean to a genuine Christian?

While American Christians are sometimes ridiculed, called names, and lied about, we are told multiplied thousands of Christians in the world are killed because of their faith in Jesus Christ ... *every single year*.

Calling Jesus their Savior and Lord meant something to them. It meant their death. Faith in Jesus often means imprisonments, loss of jobs, loss of education, loss of children, and torture and exile for hundreds of thousands of dedicated Christians in our world today.

The Bible tells us in Revelation 12:11 what it will mean to Christians in the coming day.

There are three characteristics of the Christian that will overcome this terrible temptation from the devil: "And they overcame him by:

(1) the blood of the Lamb,

(2) by the word of their testimony;

(3) and they loved not their lives unto the death."

What does this mean?

It simply means that ...

1. **Genuine Christians** have been washed and cleansed by the blood Jesus shed for man's sins on the old rugged cross. He has

become their Savior from sin and the damnation it brings.

2. **Genuine Christians** are not ashamed to praise Jesus Christ in a world that curses Him. Jesus told us that: "Whosoever therefore shall be ashamed of me and of my words in this adulterous and sinful generation; of him also shall the Son of man be ashamed, when he cometh in the glory of his Father with the holy angels." MARK 8:38

3. **Genuine Christians** will love Jesus more than life itself. **Genuine Christians** will choose to die, rather than worship anyone other than God and His only begotten Son, Jesus Christ.

Jesus told His church: "Fear none of those things which thou shalt suffer: behold, the devil shall cast some of you into prison, that ye may be tried; and ye shall have tribulation ten days: be thou faithful unto death, and I will give thee a crown of life." REVELATION 2:10

The Future Is Clear

"THE FUTURE IS CLEAR" Visa announces on the envelope containing the offer of the smart chip on a card.

Yes, it is. It is all very clear. We didn't have to wait for Visa to announce it. All we had to do was read it in God's Word, the Bible. It has already informed us of the following facts:

- **a mark will give man the right to buy and sell;**

- **where the mark will be inserted;**

- **what the mark will be used for;**

- **who will accept the mark;**

- **who will reject the mark;**

- **who, those with the mark, will worship;**

- **who, those with the mark, will blaspheme and hate;**

- **where, those with the mark, will spend their eternity.**

And oh, yes, one more thing - all who receive the mark will also be infested with a terribly grievous sore. (SEE REVELATION 16:2)

Professor Warwick was advised by his doctor to have his chip removed within ten days because of the possibility of infection. The statement issued by Reading University said: "It is therefore not known what effects it will have, how well it will operate, and how robust it will be. Professor Warwick is therefore taking an enormous risk - for the transponder to leak or shatter within his body could be catastrophic."

Current chips contain lithium. If they leak, a hole will be burned into the body. Chips are being used today to reunite lost pets with their owners and identify animals which have received vaccinations for certain diseases. The chips in animals are also supplying vital information about the effects implanted chips will have on humans. We hear so many times that new breakthroughs in medications have no adverse side effects, only to learn later that long term use of these medicines have dire and even fatal consequences. So it will be with the implanted chip.

The infectious sore, resulting from the implanted chip is prophesied in the Bible. God writes the future as easily as men pen history, with one major difference. Man writes history from his biased opinions. God states facts.

Can you now understand why there is such intense hatred and mocking ridicule for the Bible? God revealed in the Bible the enemy's specific scheme to entrap the human race! If you were the devil, wouldn't you try to suppress the publication of your best and final battle plan?

If man continues with his agenda for this coming new currency, it may not be too long before followers of Jesus Christ will have no access to the telephone system, employment, education, and all financial transactions.

It isn't too hard to imagine a world that will not allow participation in buying and selling without an implanted chip. As previously stated, Americans are not allowed presently to hold a job without a social security number, nor even to drive without a driver's license number.

How Will Christians Survive?

We don't have all the answers. In fact, we have only One. His name is Jesus.

He left this promise for His followers: "…Lo, I am with you alway, **even unto the end of the world…**" MATTHEW 28:20

I Corinthians 10:13 is a wonderful promise: "There hath no temptation taken you but such as is common to man: but God is faithful, who will not suffer you to be tempted above that ye are able; but will **with the temptation also make a way to escape**, that ye may be able to bear it."

Of course, we have a way to escape! All we need to do is to run to the Door! His name is JESUS!

"I am the door" He told us, in John 10:9!

He is the same Jesus who entered the blazing furnace with three young Hebrew men named Shadrach, Meshach and Abednego.

"Worship the golden image which I have set up," Babylon's king commanded his subjects. All but three in the entire city did.

The king gave them a second chance, but these three didn't take it. They had already made their choice. They would worship no one but God. They stood before the powerful king and declared, "Our God whom we serve is able to deliver us from the burning fiery furnace, and he will deliver us out of thine hand, O king. But if not, be it known unto thee, O king, that we will not serve thy gods, nor worship the **golden image** which thou hast set up."

God sent His Son into the furnace with these faithful young men. They emerged from the furnace without even the smell of smoke on them, as they walked past the blistered, charred corpses of the mighty soldiers the king had chosen to throw them in the furnace.

God chose to deliver them with a miracle.

They chose to worship only their God, whether He delivered them with a miracle or they died in the furnace. (FROM DANIEL, CHAPTER THREE.)

God has not changed. He is the same God who parted the Red Sea; rained manna from heaven; sent a river from a rock; dispatched an angel to cook a meal for His prophet; commanded ravens to cater bread and meat to Elijah every morning and every evening; and fed thousands from a boy's lunch.

He is also the God who demands that His followers be willing to die for Him.

Most American Christians do not have dying for Jesus on their agenda. However, we may have to do just that.

The Christian, who makes the choice today to follow Jesus wherever He leads, will faithfully follow Him through this life and right into the next.

Psalm 116:15 says, "Precious in the sight of the LORD is the death of his saints." When our loves ones leave this world for the next, we mourn and grieve our loss. Death is a wrenching experience for man. But to God ... His child is coming home. And that reunion is precious to Him.

Suffering . . . death . . . pain . . . tears.

Why does God continue to allow the people He loves to suffer? Does not John 3:16 say He loves this world? Why then does He permit the crime, the violence, the disasters, and the senseless tragedies? How can God watch soldiers die in wars and babies starve?

Don't blame God. He is not responsible for the mess man has gotten himself into. As always, we are the culprits.

God built us a splendid home. He decorated it with greenery, filled it with pools, scented it with flowers, furnished it with birds to serenade us, stocked it with good food, and buried precious metals beneath our ground. Is it His fault that we wrecked it all?

Have you chosen to blame God, because man has replaced the lullaby of frogs and the singing of birds with the screams of victims, the weeping of the diseased, and the ceaseless alarms of shrieking sirens? Some ask, "But if God's so powerful, why doesn't He fix it all?"

He already sent His only begotten, beloved Son to die in our place and deliver us from our sins.

Man tortured and crucified Him.

And once again, He is sending His Son to earth. This time, He will come, not to die, but to reign. He will "…wipe away all tears from their eyes; and there shall be no more death, neither sorrow, nor crying, neither shall there be any more pain: for the former things are passed away. And he that sat upon the throne said, "Behold, I make all things new..." REVELATION 21:4-5

God began His creation in beauty and peace, and He will restore beauty and peace through the intervention of His Son's return.

What is amazing is that the very ones who rage at God for not fixing things, will be furious with Him when He comes to fix everything. John wrote the vision he was given of this event.

"And I saw heaven opened, and behold a white horse; and he that sat upon him was called Faithful and True, and in righteousness he doth judge and make war. His eyes were as a flame of fire, and on his head were many crowns; and he had a name written, that no man knew, but he himself. And he was clothed with a vesture dipped in blood: and his name is called The Word of God. And the armies which were in heaven followed him upon white horses, clothed in fine linen, white and clean." REVELATION 19:11-14

This is the return of Jesus … coming back to repair the mess that man has made ... coming to heal the sick, stop the wars, and feed the starving babies. Is not this what we want? And yet - how will man greet our returning Creator?

"And I saw the beast, and the kings of the earth, and their armies, gathered together **to make war against him** that sat on the horse, and against his army." REVELATION 19:19

Man will greet Him with armies, weapons, and a declaration of war!

Jesus came to earth to become our Savior, and man crucified Him.

Jesus will return to earth to take His position as King of Kings and Lord of Lords, and man will declare war against Him.

The same human race that crucified our Savior will attempt to destroy our Lord. The Bible tells us the outcome of the final war. "And the beast was taken, and with him the false prophet that wrought miracles before him, with which *he deceived them that had received the mark of the beast, and them that worshipped his image.* These both were cast alive into a lake of fire burning with brimstone. And the remnant were slain with the sword ..." REVELATION 19:20-21

There it is again ... those who receive the mark of the beast are marked for final destruction at the end of this war.

You have a choice. Today is the time to make your decision.

If you fail to choose Jesus Christ by either procrastination or rejection, your destiny is sealed. This will be your future:

- You will receive the mark of the beast in your hand or in your forehead.

- You will have the right to buy and sell during the reign of the beast.

- The side effect of your implant will be a noisome *(destructive; painful)* sore.

- The wrath of God will be poured out upon you for refusing to worship Him.

- You will never again rest, but will suffer eternal torment. (READ REVELATION 14:9-11)

If your decision is to worship God by receiving His only begotten Son as your Savior and your Lord, this is your destiny.

- If you are alive when the mark of the beast is instituted, your decision may cost you your life.

- Jesus will walk with you in the fire, either sustaining you by miraculous provisions, guiding you with His wisdom, or helping you make the journey through physical death into eternal life.

The Bible tells us of the ones who made the right choice - and a multitude will! "I beheld, and, lo, a great multitude, which no man could number, of all nations, and kindreds, and people, and tongues, stood before the throne, and before the Lamb, clothed with white robes, and palms in their hands; and cried with a loud voice, saying, Salvation to our God which sitteth upon the throne, and unto the Lamb ... these are they which came out of great tribulation, and have washed their robes, and made them white in the blood of the Lamb. Therefore are they before the throne of God, and serve him day and night in his temple; and he that sitteth on the throne shall dwell among them. They shall hunger no more, neither thirst any more; neither shall the sun light on them, nor any heat. For the Lamb which is in the midst of the throne shall feed them, and shall lead them unto living fountains of waters: and God shall wipe away all tears from their eyes." (FROM REVELATION 7)

We may not be able to buy or sell soon. Yet, we have our Lord's promise that we will serve Him in the beautiful temple of God throughout all eternity.

Will you receive Jesus as your personal Savior? Will you kneel before Him, confess your sins, and ask Him for His forgiveness? Will you thank Him for giving His blood on the cross to cleanse you from your sins? Will you do this *today* - while you still have a choice? Will you then make Him your Lord, and serve Him with all your heart?

Hide the following verses in your heart! Memorize them! Live by them!

"Let your conversation be without covetousness; and be content with such things as ye have: for he hath said, I will never leave thee, nor forsake thee. So that we may boldly say, The Lord is my helper, and I will not fear what man shall do unto me." Hebrews 13:5-6

"These things I have spoken unto you, that in me ye might have peace. In the world ye shall have tribulation: but be of good cheer; I have overcome the world." JOHN 16:33

"But the hour cometh, and now is, when the true worshippers shall worship the Father in spirit and in truth: for the Father seeketh such to worship him." JOHN 4:23

Steps for Survival

1. Receive Jesus as your Savior.

2. Serve Jesus as your Lord.

3. Worship God only.

4. Be willing to die for Jesus Christ.

5. Seek God and His righteousness first.

6. Be bold in your witness of Jesus Christ. Never be ashamed of His love for you, and your love for Him!

7. Rid your life of everything that is not pleasing to God. Is there anything in your life that the devil could use as bait to entice you to take the mark? If you cannot get victory over a sin, an addiction, or a habit now - how will you get victory then?

Jeremiah 12:5 says: "If thou hast run with the footmen, and they have wearied thee, then how canst thou contend with horses...?"

Eve lived in a perfect garden, where she and Adam walked and talked with the Lord daily. She was told that she could eat freely of every tree - except one. Yet she yielded to Satan's temptation and was lured into the serpent's trap. God's provision was not enough for her.

Genesis 3:1 describes the serpent as "more subtil than any beast of the field". This same **subtil beast** will entice men in the end days. Genesis 3:6 tells us why Eve chose to disobey God: "And when the woman saw that the tree was ...

(1) **good for food**, and that it was

(2) **pleasant to the eyes**, and a tree

(3) **to be desired to make one wise**,

she took of the fruit thereof, and did eat, and gave also unto her husband with her; and he did eat."

You may say that you would not have yielded. But is that true? Each time that we turn away from God's will to do our will or the devil's will, we are repeating Eve's sin.

Study I John 2:15-18, while examining yourself: "Love not the world, neither the things that are in the world. If any man love the world, the love of the Father is not in him. For all that is in the world, **the lust of the flesh**, and **the lust of the eyes**, and **the pride of life**, is not of the Father, but is of the world. And the world passeth away, and the lust thereof: but he that doeth the will of God abideth for ever. Little children, it is the last time: and as ye have heard that antichrist shall come, even now are there many antichrists; whereby we know that it is the last time."

Did you notice that the "old serpent" uses the same old bait?

He came to Eve with the offer of good food.

He comes today and offers the lust of the flesh.

He will come tomorrow to offer the right to buy and sell to satisfy the lust of the flesh.

He came to Eve offering fruit that was pleasant to the eyes.

He comes today to appeal to the lust of the eyes.

He will come tomorrow to offer all the things that look good to us!

He came to Eve with the promise to make her wise.

He comes today to appeal to man's pride of life.

He will come tomorrow to offer superior wisdom through the implanted chip.

Esau sold his birthright for one bowl of soup. If you have been born again, don't sell your spiritual birthright!

Judas was one of twelve apostles who walked and talked with Jesus. He traded his apostleship for 30 pieces of silver – then he went and hanged himself.

The rich young ruler walked away from Jesus' call for one reason: he loved his possessions more than he loved God. He chose to lose what he could have kept eternally, in order to keep what he would forever lose.

Ask the Lord today to take everything out of your life that would cause you to be ensnared by Satan. Submit yourself totally to God. He alone will be your strength in these end days!

John **6:66** is a sobering verse that should cause us to examine our walk with God. "From that time many of his disciples went back, and walked no more with him."

Many today profess Christianity – but Christ does not possess them. And once again, there will be many who will walk no more with Him.

Fate of the Beast and False Prophet

"And I saw the beast, and the kings of the earth, and their armies, gathered together to make war against him that sat on the horse, and against his army. And the beast was taken, and with him the false prophet that wrought miracles before him, with which he deceived them that had received the mark of the beast, and them that worshipped his image. These both were cast alive into a lake of fire burning with brimstone."
REVELATION 19:19-20

Fate of the Devil

"And the devil that deceived them was cast into the lake of fire and brimstone, where the beast and the false prophet are, and shall be tormented day and night for ever and ever." REVELATION 20:10

Fate of Recipients of the Mark of the Beast

"And I heard a great voice out of the temple saying to the seven angels, Go your ways, and pour out the vials of the wrath of God upon the earth. And the first went, and poured out his vial upon the earth; and there fell a noisome and grievous sore upon the men which had the mark of the beast, and upon them which worshipped his image." REVELATION 16:1-2

"And the third angel followed them, saying with a loud voice, If any man worship the beast and his image, and receive his mark in his forehead, or in his hand, the same shall drink of the wine of the wrath of God, which is poured out without mixture into the cup of his indignation; and he shall be tormented with fire and brimstone in the presence of the holy angels, and in the presence of the Lamb: and the smoke of their torment ascendeth up for ever and ever: and they have no rest day nor night, who worship the beast and his image, and whosoever receiveth the mark of his name." REVELATION 14:9-11

Promises to the Victorious

"And I saw as it were a sea of glass mingled with fire: and them that had gotten the victory over the beast, and over his image, and over his mark, and over the number of his name, stand on the sea of glass, having the harps of God. And they sing the song of Moses the servant of God, and the song of the Lamb, saying, Great and marvellous are thy works, Lord God Almighty; just and true are thy ways, thou King of saints."
REVELATION 15:2-3

"And I saw thrones, and they sat upon them, and judgment was given unto them: and I saw the souls of them that were beheaded for the witness of Jesus, and for the word of God, and which had not worshipped the beast, neither his image, neither had received his mark upon their foreheads, or in their hands; and they lived and reigned with Christ a thousand years. But the rest of the dead lived not again until the thousand years were finished. This is the first resurrection. Blessed and holy is he that hath part in the first resurrection: on such the second death hath no power, but they shall be priests of God and of Christ, and shall reign with him a thousand years." REVELATION 20:4-6

The Approaching Night

Jesus said: "...the night cometh, when no man can work." JOHN 9:4

How can such a night come? Can we not at least pray for our lost loved ones? Our prayers would avail nothing. If they have taken the mark, their destiny is already sealed. Neither our witness, nor our prayers, will accomplish anything in the coming day of darkness.

The time to reach souls for Christ is **today**. It is not enough that we receive this warning ourselves. If we love others, we will warn them of danger ahead! If we are true disciples of Christ, we will obey His commandments. He said, "If ye love me, keep my commandments." JOHN 14:15

I John 2:3-5 says: "And hereby we do know that we know him, if we keep his commandments. He that saith, I know him, and keepeth not his commandments, is a liar, and the truth is not in him. But whoso keepeth his word, in him verily is the love of God perfected: hereby know we that we are in him."

What are His commandments?

Jesus also said: "...Thou shalt love the Lord thy God with all thy heart, and with all thy soul, and with all thy mind. This is the first and great commandment. And the second is like unto it, Thou shalt love thy neighbour as thyself. On these two commandments hang all the law and the prophets."
MATTHEW 22:37-40

If we obey the first commandment, and love **THE <u>LORD</u> – <u>OUR</u> GOD** – with all our heart, soul, and mind – we will surely not bow to this world and worship one who is anti-(against) Christ!

And are we keeping our Lord's second commandment? Jesus said that we are to love our neighbors as ourselves! How can we love others, yet withhold the gospel and the warnings in the Bible from them?

If we truly love others, we will want them to make Christ their Savior and heaven their home, just as much as we desire these blessings for ourselves.

Our love will cause us to do everything we can do – now – to introduce men, women, and children to our Savior! Our love will cause us to do everything that we can do – now – to warn them of the coming chip and its consequences!

Christ's love for us moved Him from heaven to earth - from the manger to the cross - just so we could be saved from sin and dwell in heaven forever.

Will your love for others move you to obey Christ's command to: "...Go ye into all the world, and preach the gospel to every creature"? (MARK 16:15)

Do You Have an Ear?

The book of Revelation gives us the following command in seven verses, in chapters 2 & 3: "He that hath an ear, *let him hear* what the Spirit saith unto the churches." The message is repeated, in Revelation 13:9: "If any man have an ear, *let him hear*."

Many do not have ears to hear the warnings of God. We have been told by pastors that they were taught in seminaries not to preach from the book of Revelation. Yet, it is the one book that promises a blessing to all who hear or read it – and keep it! Listen to this beautiful promise, in the first three verses of the book of Revelation:

"The Revelation of Jesus Christ, which God gave unto him, *to shew unto his servants things which must shortly come to pass*; and he sent and signified it by his angel unto his servant John: who bare record of the word of God, and of the testimony of Jesus Christ, and of all things that he saw. **Blessed is he that readeth, and they that hear the words of this prophecy, and keep those things which**

are written therein: for the time is at hand."

We are warned in I Thessalonians 5:20: "Despise not prophesyings."

God wants us to be aware! If He didn't, these prophecies would not be in the Bible!

Christ's disciples did not want to hear what would happen to Him, when He bodily walked this earth - but He told them anyway!

Can you imagine their shock, as they listened to His words for the first time: "From that time forth began Jesus to shew unto his disciples, how that he must go unto Jerusalem, and suffer many things of the elders and chief priests and scribes, and be killed, and be raised again the third day. Then Peter took him, and began to rebuke him, saying, Be it far from thee, Lord: this shall not be unto thee. But he turned, and said unto Peter, Get thee behind me, Satan: thou art an offence unto me: for thou savourest not the things that be of God, but those that be of men." MATTHEW 16:21-23

Can you imagine them seeing their Master - the Water Walker, Dead Raiser, Leper Healer, Storm Calmer – being arrested, beaten, and crucified, without having been warned that it would happen?

Do we not want to be warned by a siren that an ambulance is speeding toward us? Do we not want to be warned that a tornado is approaching our city? Do we not want to be warned that a hurricane is raging toward our coast? Do swimmers not want to be warned of a dangerous riptide? Do we not want the authorities to warn us that a deranged shooter is in our school?

Paul wrote of Satan, in II Corinthians 2:11: "...we are not ignorant of his devices."

We need to listen to our Lord's warning, in Luke 21:34-36: "And take heed to yourselves, lest at any time your hearts be overcharged with surfeiting, and drunkenness, and cares of this life, and **so that day come upon you un**awares. For as **a snare** shall it come on all them that dwell on the face of the whole earth. **Watch** ye therefore, and **pray always**, that ye may be accounted worthy to **escape** all these things that shall come to pass, and to stand before the Son of man."

How foolish it is to bury our heads in the sand and not look up until we hear the glorious sound of the trumpet, announcing Jesus' return.

For our own sakes and for our children's sakes, should we not be alert? We do not hesitate to warn them of wearing seatbelts or making friends with strangers. Should we not then warn our children of the dangers that threaten their eternal souls?

Our Lord loves us! He has told us what is coming, so we can be prepared, rather than shocked!

If you are one who has an ear – listen to the warnings that are in God's Word!

Be Strong In the Lord!

"Finally, my brethren, **be strong in the Lord**, and in the power of **his might**. Put on the whole armour of God, that ye may be able to **stand against the wiles of the devil**. For we wrestle not against flesh and blood, but against principalities, against powers, against the rulers of the darkness of this world, against spiritual wickedness in high places. Wherefore take unto you the whole armour of God, that ye may be able to **withstand in the evil day,** and having done all, to stand. Stand therefore, having your loins girt about with truth, and having on the breastplate of righteousness; And your feet shod with the preparation of the gospel of peace; Above all, taking the shield of faith, wherewith ye shall be able to quench all the fiery darts of the wicked. And take the helmet of salvation, and the sword of the Spirit, which is the word of God: Praying always with all prayer and supplication in the Spirit, and watching thereunto with all perseverance and supplication for all saints."
EPHESIANS 6:10-18

"…the people that do know their God shall be strong, and do exploits." DANIEL 11:32

Jesus said:

"**Whosoever will come after me,
let him deny himself,
and take up his cross,
and follow me.
For whosoever will save his life
shall lose it;
but whosoever shall lose his life
for my sake and the gospel's,
the same shall save it.
For what shall it profit a man,
if he shall gain the whole world,
and lose his own soul?
Or what shall a man give
in exchange for his soul?**"

MARK 8:34-37

"Now unto him that is able to keep you from falling, and to present you faultless before the presence of his glory with exceeding joy, to the only wise God our Saviour, be glory and majesty, dominion and power, both now and ever. Amen."
JUDE 1:24-25

"But thanks be to God, which giveth us the victory through our Lord Jesus Christ."
I CORINTHIANS 15:57

SOUND THE TRUMPET!

"BLOW YE THE TRUMPET IN ZION, AND SOUND AN ALARM IN MY HOLY MOUNTAIN: LET ALL THE INHABITANTS OF THE LAND TREMBLE: FOR THE DAY OF THE LORD COMETH, FOR IT IS NIGH AT HAND." JOEL 2:1

"Son of man, speak to the children of thy people, and say unto them, When I bring the sword upon a land, if the people of the land take a man of their coasts, and set him for their watchman: If when he seeth the sword come upon the land, he blow the trumpet, and warn the people; then whosoever heareth the sound of the trumpet, and taketh not warning; if the sword come, and take him away, his blood shall be upon his own head. He heard the sound of the trumpet, and took not warning; his blood shall be upon him. But he that taketh warning shall deliver his soul.

"But if the watchman see the sword come, and blow not the trumpet, and the people be not warned; if the sword come, and take any person from among them, he is taken away in his iniquity; but his blood will I require at the watchman's hand." Ezekiel 33:2-6

Paul Wilde, and his wife, Carolyn, reside in Foley, Alabama, where he is Pastor of:

NEW LIFE IN CHRIST CHURCH
102 E. Berry Avenue
Foley, Alabama 36535
Telephone: (251) 943-2225

Web Site: www.newlifeinchristchurch.net
Email: pcwilde@gulftel.com

A Complete List of the books and Home Bible Courses by Paul and Carolyn Wilde is on the Church Web Site.

"I must work the works of him that sent me, while it is day: the night cometh, when no man can work."

"Watchman! What of the night?"

JOHN 9:4 AND ISAIAH 21:11

RECENT HEADLINES & ARTICLES

MICROCHIP MIND CONTROL, IMPLANTS, AND CYBERNETICS

BY RAUNI-LEENA LUUKANEN-KILDE, MD

FORMER CHIEF MEDICAL OFFICER OF FINLAND

With the help of satellites, the implanted person can be tracked anywhere on the globe. When a 5-micro-millimeter microchip (the diameter of a strand of hair is 50 micromillo-meters) is placed into (the) optical nerve of the eye, it draws neuroimpulses from the brain that embody the experiences, smells, sights and voice of the implanted person. Once transferred and stored in a computer, these neuroimpulses can be projected back to the person's brain via the microchip to be re-experienced.

CHINA JOINS THE GLOBAL PUSH FOR CASHLESS SOCIETY

Editor: **Technocracy News & Trends**

Technocracy demands total digital control over the entire global economy, and this cannot be achieved until cash has been completely driven out; this war on cash is already evident on every continent in the world, and it is not to be taken lightly!

"We need a program of psychosurgery and political control of our society. The purpose is physical control of the mind. Everyone who deviates from the given norm can be SURGICALLY MUTILATED."

DARPA

The Defense Advanced Research Projects Agency (DARPA) is in the process of making a neural-coding device capable of controlling artificial limbs when seeded in the brain. The Pentagon has subsidized the institution $62 million to help foster this mind-control technology. Meanwhile, the **mainstream media is pushing for the microchipping of children sooner rather than later.**

DARPA is already working on microchips that can be implanted into soldiers' brains to make them more resilient to warfare.

SMARTPHONE OF THE FUTURE WILL BE IN YOUR BRAIN - CNN

THOUSANDS OF PEOPLE IN SWEDEN GET MICROCHIP IMPLANTS FOR A NEW WAY OF LIFE
SMALL IMPLANTS WERE FIRST USED IN 2015 IN SWEDEN AND SINCE THEN PEOPLE HAVE BECOME ACTIVE IN MICROCHIPPING

SOUTH CHINA MORNING POST: EDITION: HONG KONG
PUBLISHED: Sunday, 13 May, 2018

Sweden's SJ national railway company has won over some 130 users to its microchip reservation service in a year. Conductors scan passengers' hands after they book tickets online and register them on their chip. Twenty-eight year-old Ulrika Celsing is one of 3,000 Swedes to have injected a microchip into her hand to try out a new way of life. When Celsing's innovatively minded media company organized an event where employees could get the implants, she followed the crowd. She said she felt nothing but a slight sting when the syringe inserted the chip into her left hand, which she now uses on an almost daily basis and does not fear hacking or possible surveillance. "I don't think our current technology is enough to get chip hacked. But I may think about this again in the future. I could always take it out then," she says.

However, for Ben Libberton, a microbiologist working for MAX IV Laboratory in the southern city of Lund which provides X-rays for research, the danger is real. The chip implants could cause "infections or reactions of the immune system", he warned. "The more data (that) is stored in a single place, as could happen with a chip, the more risk it could be used against us."

42978389R00064

Made in the USA
Middletown, DE
20 April 2019